Also by Michael Goldman

FIRST POEMS (1965)

AT THE EDGE

AT THE EDGE

Poems by Michael Goldman

The Macmillan Company

Collier-Macmillan Ltd., London

ACKNOWLEDGMENTS

Some of the poems in this collection first appeared in the following magazines and anthology to whose editors grateful acknowledgment is made: *The Massachusetts Review, Prairie Schooner, The Kenyon Review, The Nation.* The poem "The Visitor" first appeared in *The New Yorker*; the poem "The Probes" was first published in the anthology *Of Poetry & Power*, Basic Books, Inc., 1964.

FIRST PRINTING

The Macmillan Company
Collier-Macmillan Canada Ltd., Toronto, Ontario
Printed in the United States of America

for Eleanor

CONTENTS

I

II

III

IV

I

NEWS

The edge is where a fist
mourns, the street
is eaten out with bits of glass or silver;
the arm suddenly glass
is out there, finished . . .
There is a film over the photograph;
a fish that has lived too long on wastes
rises to the pier.
Close to us, fading, being eaten from below,
it spreads out under the surface like paper.

AN OBSERVER

I picked the red ant up and let him run
on a square sheet of glass.
I watched him, I bent like tall grass.
He scattered to the edges, then cut back.
I was far away from him, a young mountain.
My legs sank below us, deep in their armies of hair.

ROUTINES

Long letters come here from my friends, the loveliest thing
    in the world.
I am a sailor who has rented a jungle.
Every now and then I put in a couple of seeds.

Yes folks,
my guest tomorrow morning
will be me.

                Every little image
                has a meaning all its own
                there's an author just inside me
                and he wants to use the phone

"I really wonder about you"

                    Drink it
                    the moon reads
                    our wet leaves
                    all night
                    the matted grass
                    bites
                    drink it

Is there something you want me to understand
something I'm supposed to guess

            Don't let me
            I'm getting
            out of bed
            want to know where

I put my head
want to know who
got killed last night
don't want to let you
out of my sight
Don't let me
Don't let me

We each were waiting, lying together
in city summer
the waste of first light
to be packaged

I said nothing

She later
married a queer
her own sex
so difficult
electric
along her mouth

Am I imagining things?
What if—

FOOL YOUR FRIENDS
LEARN TO THROW YOUR VOICE

"Connaissez-vous le Upper West Side?"

Over the Tuscan hills with their fresh trees, the shadow
of a hill rises. We ride the highway through them
like vanilla. We pass
an old man sleeping on his cart.
Spring. It is easy to like it.

I wrote three letters this morning
sitting in the garden with coffee
at a pink stone table,
cool stone softened with yellow light.
I described the old iron gate, the poplars waking
    with birds,
the distant hills, the pink stone, etc.

What do you think of the news?

        The Moderate Nationalists
        have eaten a nun.

Can you tell us what this show meant? Ay, or any other
    show.

"She's interested in me," Gladheart said, "the one on the
Rue Mouffetard, she's very intelligent. Didn't you see the
way she looked at me? The whores here are something
special—we've had amazing conversations. This place is
alive, man, it really hallucinates. Listen, I'm writing on
Henry Miller and Goebbels." He reached under the bed
and brought out a sheaf of manuscript. He gestured wildly:
Hasidic light danced in his eyes. "Sperm-consciousness,
that's what this city has. The Seine is nothing but sperm,
night and diamonds. You know there's no sperm in American literature? Oh, they've been putting in a little lately,
but it's all evaporated and crusty . . ."

Two mornings a week I get up in the dark.
My house is 30 miles from the main town.
I teach English conversation and general culture.

        The water
        ink blue
        below us

7

white sand
and the olive trees
fighting
through the hills

I enclose a snapshot

Caught in my lights,
frightened pigs
on the mudflats

You accused me. But what was I after? I wanted to put my
fingers under my belly, pull out the nerves one by one,
twist them like threads to a single rope, and hold its tip
against you till there was a burst of fire and I could feel
the gentle trembling and warmth. Normality sweet as a
perversion: modern love. And you had something hidden
under your tongue. An undeveloped thought or tumor, a
piece of poignant obstruction lodged in our common tubes.
Blockage, a nightmare of tenderness. We said goodbye in
the subway, dreaming of the Metro. The whole world—
legs, insurrection, a student ship riding at night through
the North Sea—shimmered with adorable farewells. Sunset
on moldy churches, lovely as literature. Lost opportunities,
our universal theme.

I understand now that I did not know you, will never
know you, was incapable of knowing you. You gave me a
body voluptuous with my diseases. Now it sleeps in the
body of this island, under the hot wall with its ivy and
swollen figs, convalescing like a lizard in the sun. Drink,
say the oracles; no wonder we are bewildered. Tomorrow,
start again.

To stay in one place and fight
like a tree for its air

My autograph?

The country night
blackened with stars.

SANDPIPER

Where he is frail and runs
in the glistening what-is-left
the Atlantic
pulls back
into its blackness.
He runs on thin sticks
leaving arrows.
Off now
swinging out
where the night clouds in—
thoughts glimpsed in music but not held—
he planes and rises.
What we lose each day comes back
in raked staves and shattered horseshoe crabs,
bolts of dried grass return
under the day-wing;
the beach opens forever,
littered, shining.

A PICTURE IN THE NEWS

The cop clutches
a growth near his heart

black, tiny,
killing us.

SAFETY FIRST

Aristotle's firm voice tells us that poetry
must be judged in moral terms.
—from a recent essay by an American poet

Aristotle's firm voice—
two donuts to each sailor;
the destroyer plunges forward full of excitement.

I see a poet plowing in a field.
The field is white; it is heaped with magazines.
He tells his friends, Welcome to the Pampas!

He tells me about Aristotle's firm voice.
The sailors will need large gray poetry,
poetry like a ship that has been lost for a year in the Andes,
that floats but will not shoot.

It has been a long day.
I stop at the drugstore for a package of peace tablets.
A blind Negro sells me a copy of the *Daily Peace.*
My gentle father-in-law stands in the street with blood on
      his collar
reciting O TASTE AND PEACE and the PEACE
      CANTOS.

When I get home there is a message waiting, "Call
      Aristotle."
As a precaution against fire I eat the paper.

OUR SILENCE

We are drinking; the silence
moves like a fish in my glass.
I stir it, feeling for a clear place
but the room has filled to a place
where self stops, as breathing
drowns in sleep or a streetlight
stares emptily at midnight, and another
self, that drinks the room's darkness,
governs our silence like a tide.

THE VISITOR

Heavy with length of days, summer continues.
The grass is blanketed with little burrs.
A bottle of insects whispers and stirs at the window.
The rain is over.
Time waits in the tremor of a leaf,
and one night, in the first grayness,
the lake's still gaze is broken:
a schoolboy wakens to the end of things;
a tall bird stands at the shore.

AN EDGE

The brush comes up to us;
we hear
everything that moves.

Under the shiny bushes—
dry leaves.

A bird is scratching through it
like wolves.

All over the hot sky
there are cries and calls
like calligraphy, like little worms;

it is
a scratchiness, a dryness
we could drink
like juice
in the wires,
switches we brush in our mouths
when we taste wine.
A frightened snake
dives for his rock;
in this house, in the woods,
there is a chance of fire,
a liquid, an edge like a nerve
buried for miles.

VERY SLOWLY

This boat is going somewhere.
The surface is oil-green.
The wind is from my left, very light,
but the boat goes ahead.
Late sun, pollen on the water,
a leaf eases past me.
The water must be flowing out.

This tree tore loose last night;
its head is down in the water.
The leafy branches arch like a swimmer's arms
and go under.

Now I am in with the rocks
the flooded lake has half-covered.
I take up my paddle and slow down.
Backwater, backwater, I make her turn;
we have stopped behind the floating trunk.
A turtle gazes stupidly ahead.
Out in the middle of the lake
something jumps.

FOR ANDREI VOZNESENSKY
(AND THE WRITERS' UNION)

In June of 1967, Voznesensky was pre-vented by the Soviet Writers' Union from attending a poetry festival in New York; he cabled its sponsors, "Can't come." The Union's action, in this case, seems to have been prompted less by political interference from outside than by certain members' long-standing enmity toward Voznesensky.

Because you couldn't come
my car skidded.
My pen was covered with a sticky gum;
I was bitten by horseflies, the lake was too cold.

Because you couldn't come
the news got worse;
the police appeared all night smiling and kicking;
a bar of soap addressed us; it said, "Drink more gasoline."

Because you couldn't come
everything organized;
The National Council of Sparrows drove with their lights
　　　　on;
The Faculty of Philosophy bought a moon.

Because you couldn't come
500 poets
mimeographed their complete works as a form of protest;
we rented a p.a. system, we danced in front of City Hall.

Because you couldn't come
we got excited.

We were nervous with all the microphones and lights
but what a breakthrough it was—delirium! makeup!
    sweaters!

Because you couldn't come
we made mistakes.
We thought it was New York, but we were underwater;
we thought mushrooms were wheat, we combed our hair
    with frogs.

Because you couldn't come
we forgot things;
there was no grass in our poetry, no people,
no mosquitoes, moss, radios, linen, rubies—
just little pieces of paper with names at the bottom.

Because you couldn't come
it was hot.
Because you couldn't come when the railroads struck,
when the teachers struck, when the lights failed, when the
    Negroes,
the moonbeams, the Catholics, the critics, the pavements,
    the welfare and the newsreels
became just too much, somebody had to denounce you.
We had no choice.
Do you think you're the only one with feeling, technique,
    problems?

Because you couldn't come
a bunch of my friends
asked me to help kick this big balloon figure.
They told me it was President Johnson, but I think it
    was you.

FINISH

I put her through seven revisions; she was fine.

I put her through eight more, and she said,
"You will never be completely mine."

I had to help her through the next fifteen.
You see what I mean?

II

DRINKING

I come up through this beer
with seaweed on my lips.
Look, there's land out there
rocking in the mist.
I am the waves, I.
The coast is big and green.
Your little boat is coming out to meet me.
Delicate tourist,
I know your tricks.

SUMMER AFTERNOON

A gray man in a page of mist
rises above the river towards New Jersey.
Energy is trapped where we cannot see—
on the lost shore a green sleeper
slowly eats his houses.
The air is filling, cooling;
night is coming, with its heavy stars.

MOVING DEEPER

In the scrolls of rough leaves,
black-green, touching thorn,
edging our sides forward, parting
bush-trunk, grass-stalk, branches
of scrolled leaves, the dark
with long snakes of sunlight
dangling through,
the push of our steps is clear and soft.
A bird cracks past us.
Moving deeper, we make our way.

THE DAISY

A flower white as the news;
in high grass, one petal
eaten away.
A flea jumps from its eye.
A whorl of yellow heads
is the center,
dark egg-yolk color.

Today I think the meaning is—no effort;
just shape, clearness, freshness,
a sweep from center to center
like alder smell or percolating coffee
or stubbing your toe.

The stalk is smooth as a weed
with its ladder of blunt leaves;
like a young reporter in a movie—
no effort, but on the spot,
and that crazy head, like nothing.

For three hours in the morning
while the air is still a little cool,
you can step outside and breathe.
This is the daisy, aiming
to be tougher than all police,
a mountain summer waking in your lungs.
We look up through the gala oaks;
the air is chattering, heating,
the sky is a blue telephone receiver.
We have rented the weather.
Like summer or the morning mail
we've arrived.

CHANGING EVERYTHING

I want to be dull and keep you
by the dull presence of my shoulders.
I want to come into your room with nothing to say
and change everything.
The world turns away like a family.
Will you help me get back to it?
You go on sitting
quiet as the world.

YOUTH

A bad storm crowding the bay;
the leaves blew silver and a weight fell
through the air: youth.
I ran through the vines and creepers by the shore
while the fat drops touched me and I broke
green pears in the tall grass.

And now I touch the summer
of ideas. Boss only
of the flooded interior, I come home,
the sun pulled down behind the river.
Orange light floods my back
and youth's great building swings its door.

Night grows in my apartment.
Here are the flowers, the chair arrangements.
The rug thickens and the wood glows deeply;
a white scar has risen in the ceiling.
The windows hum; above me
something is being dragged along the floor.

TOTAL DESTRUCTION

Total destruction. I wish I could grasp the idea.
When I go out for breakfast I can look up
and see a gray apartment building 15 stories high.
How if that grimy cornice, in which I can already see a
      crack,
were to break off, drop on my head
and smash my brains out onto the sidewalk?
                                      That would be
partial destruction, I suppose.

NOW ALL THE WATERS

Now all the waters
fall through the houses,
breaking the morning,
breaking the floors,
insect voices
rise on the wiring;
now all the waters,
the showers, the static,
angelic plumbing,
finish, finish;
the city flushes
itself to the ocean,
the strong doors smash,
the news continues;
I am the announcer
please hear me, please hear me,
all that the waters
finish is finished.
Surrender, surrender.

IN THE WOODS

"I grew like hair to your clothes."
In the woods, red ivy marked the way.
The ants streamed with nervous terror.
My hand fled over her breasts like a vine.

THE BLESSING

It is mild winter in Washington;
a big ear blossoms through the fog.
What are they saying? Is it
mistakes, sewage, a mother?
I see a woman choking on her hair
and the mild crowds flowing away.

But the Capitol stones transmit;
they are radios for the nation
and the voice of my First Lady
shakes the chambers, "A poet!
What this country needs is a poet
to grab my hair and make the snakes stop."

Her fists pound at her ears. Stop!
"I have set fire to my husband for culture,
torn up my scalp and my dresses,
thwarted my children, and now
I break through the stones like a tree
shaking my red buds to the river."

Her lips still love me, her mouth
that tastes of milk and ashes—
what a strain, what a delusion:
to be a mother to poets!
Her skin is gray with trying.
I must join her in public.

Why did she wait so long? I can't
bear these needs, this nakedness.
Always too much—and now I have to fly

over the poles, over the jungles.
I will give readings in Chicago
and change things quietly for her.

Then I will live in Europe
or a town house in silver New York
where night lights up the fountains
and money and play rise speaking
to the bleached Plaza trees and that
reached, irresponsible moon.

MORNING POEM

Sun at a distance, a cool telegram;
the grass is fine, there is a grub in it,
a spider; the air is still quite cold.

I hear what she said when you smile about it
as the mind hears its absence through the cedars,
as we hear,

through the far-off smashing of the sea,
wind over the caves, a girl's voice,
or a river, racing to be drowned.

III

STAYING ON

He knew what would happen—something would go
and suddenly his face would change.
Then there would be nothing but a staying on
as at the beach at the end of summer,
a walk on the day of leaving in an old sweater,
a very clear day.

Walking on, spreading the dry sand, waiting
to turn around and walk back;
he sat at his desk and the air like a mirror contained him.

THE PROPHET

Motte in neat old clothes,
the man with the flag,
stands on the little chair, angry,
the agent of God.
I lose you in Motte and the streets.

Where are we now, speaking,
the wind shoving the streets?
God is speaking,
the power of mind is speaking.
My hands look for you under a car.

IL MAESTRO

An eminent Italian writer is spending the summer on the Mediterranean, near the mouth of a river. He is visited by a recurrent dream. During the course of the poem he works on a manuscript, begins a letter to a friend, and makes various mental and written notes.

"Brightness of the flesh that forms
over scars, the river pale,
color of the olive leaf
beaten upward by a storm . . .

Dearest Friend,
It is twenty years since the war, twenty years since those
      nightmares—
my competition, I called them. But my rival is back,
and he has changed. Now with ironic fluency he sends me
a woman with a lined face, sad, immensely desirable,
a woman who may be forty, who may be fifty . . ."

I

Every night the old poet
sleeps in his beach house, hears the river
advancing a woman with hair like weed
over the rocks to the green ocean.

He looks at an ancient photograph, it is all there;
the years departing through the light or dark,
figures along a shore, "the language of Dante."
He takes a little corner and writes it down.

The new girl is in Rome, the war is a black rock
covered by vines, mounted by trees.
He breathes; he feels a melon in his heart.
She is nineteen; "I am heaving like a donkey."

Near morning, heat lightning flashes in the west—
"The blank sea, rocks damp with weeds;
myself one image among many resources."
His furniture shines in the airy dark.

II

He walks at midday along the beach;
alphabets dry on the stone—
"an inspector of small shells, poker of crabs,"
Neptune on a visit to the front.

Two planes are climbing the sky—slow trails,
the high line of greatness, the low one of exhaustion.
They cross and each goes on.
Finally the world became vocabulary.

"A man leaving middle age, waiting for lunch,
alone on a hot beach, still a lover,
a man who enjoys white wine, whose photograph
is known in many cities," who sleeps less and less . . .

The face of the woman in his dreams, her hair . . .
She grew close, like the end of fighting in the city—
lime-scent clung on the wind, in his mouth a taste of
        metal—
a body offering its defeated fullness.

An aging woman loosened for his pleasure—
Yes; she was the final version of success:
easy death, naked after the war,
lucky to find him, grateful to be used.

HER NIGHT-THOUGHTS

I

"I want to live wastefully, carelessly,
a lit cigarette in a blacked-out city.
Come to me at the night's end;
I see myself on a sofa
where the ashes have spilled and the wine
spills from a green bottle.
I want everything spilled in my room,
my knees are up, my head
propped on the sofa-arm. Outside
I want to hear the tires.
The streets are empty;
a dirty light begins."

II

"It is so hard to be like this.
I feel as if I had spent each day for years
building an ocean out of nail-parings.
The air feels thin, heavy and thin;
I wish I could suck more of it in.
Leaning back, I feel I could be filled
by a granular muscle, huge, as big as this room,
bigger than me. Could I write about that?
My mind
seems full of old October afternoons
and sunshine on the wheat in Normandy.
What can I do?
Night again. Trouble. Shoes. A few good lines.
I lift a bunch of poppies to the moon.
I stretch and yawn my golden sides.

I wish for a muscle
that would fill me up . . .
My father has a cramp in an ocean of gasoline.
Boxes of horrible music are carried by."

A STYLE

Finished, it has a gleam
that covers and clarifies its freckles like marble
or at moments
is like a rich clear glass through which the light comes
    slowly.
It is limited, like an epitaph,
to being clear and kind.

ADVICE

You came up, with drink beginning to get to you
like news of a victory and revealed to me
the secrets of poetry. "Be a monster,"
you said, "keep them guessing.
Keep them saying, what's Goldman up to now?"
Then you moved on to the party's deeper reaches. I stuck
in a little eddy of guests, meeting several people
whose names I recognized. Later,
you rose up in the corner with arms like dragon-wings
and we all vanished.
I wondered what either of us might do
to change.

THE PROBES

after an assassination

Let us section his nude body
into five stages,
each by a cut through the groin.

The eye that seems to stare at you
from the open hip is
illusion; it is a slice of your eye.

The choric knotting of these dark ropes
is like slow thinking;
we reach the chipped bulges of the joints.

The massive thigh-bone now, the temple, the great
hangar of the chest, the
facial plane stripped clean by a rotary saw.

Here the examining knife
comes on softness, on
pockets of fluid that explode.

An arm borne by the sewage!
Heart's splendor;
a king's mouth smashed to grinning rocks.

Quickly we return to the scrape of metal
over bone. The wiping-up
continues. I feel the

cool touch of a sponge on the back of my neck.
What do you feel?
Do you feel we have just about covered the subject?

Then let us finish off our operations
neatly by felicitating
Language—who has survived so many changes

of state, of policy, of conversation,
with no loss to herself. It's so
swell to feel superior, even to a nation.

ORPHEUS

Between two lines of print
a voice is tearing.
Newspaper ink spreads on the tips of my fingers.

I pull towards me, making the fine sound.
It is a falls, a whisper,
a stretch of giving like the shout of a distant crowd.

There is a sharpness to it, a note like fat burning.
Even thinking
gets into it, this stripping between facts.

It is the news of a last speech.
Tall women
run through the high grass towards bloody water.

AT THE INCINERATOR

The squirrel raises his tan head tenderly
and runs his narrow tongue over the bricks for garbage.
We watch him from the bathroom window;
my wife hands me the binoculars.
When the Muse comes She doesn't tell you to write;
She says get up for a minute, I've something to show you,
stand here.

A PHOTOGRAPH OF THEODORE ROETHKE

A wall of white shadowy light, flowers, bee-motion,
his face blazingly lit before it, laughter
opening a dark mouth, teeth and flowers,
a big naked throat, a hood—black—thrown back,
the whole bulky overall too black to make out
and down in the corner
the bright, thick hands thrown crosswise at right angles
driving out of the picture. The laughter
carries us back to the mouth, the teeth mixed up with the
       flowers,
the nose a roaring boy's, a chipmunk pouch to the cheek,
a big forking vein under the ear,
the skin a puckering arrow lodged at the crease of the eye,
age forming on the laughter, the light caking like makeup,
pain coming to life. He entertains it;
he hugs his body. Bees fly out of his mouth.

A BOOK IN THE MORNING

Warmed in the belly,
the light gaining,
smoothing with coffee,
the oak leaves massing,
mist over the ridges,
I put down my cup.
Read. Stop reading.
A deer snorted on my right.
Head turned, he stares at me, ready to run;
but nothing registers and, lovely,
he's back to his mushrooms.
A cool rainy breeze shifts everything.
I pick up the book, breathing in
laurel, cold lake, honeysuckle,
waking up. The words on the next page
may be alive.

LISTENING

I hear a shaking of chips,
a high clash repeated in the air
off in the hot woods,
and your electric typewriter
near me on the porch.

Back on the base of my spine
I am balanced in a cool corner,
windows on both sides
my notebook on my lap.
I feel nicely stopped
while everything else goes on.
                              Of course,
my skin goes on, my pants are wearing out,
my heart, too, I suppose, while my shoulders
are still getting stronger and my mind
is different every day. My body is more
here every year, it is dying and waking up.
In a minute I will go back to my crazy work.

Now the insect has stopped.
Marriage too is a mystery.
You type—think—type.
We are part of life.

THASOS

The water
ink blue
below us
white sand
and the olive trees
storming down
all the way
in turbulence
like lovely police
gray-green
in a photograph
going into action
against the emptiness.

SWINGING

A golf swing,
thorny rose—
fastened tight to the soil,
unfolding.
It's tough to keep low when you're swinging;
floating is useless,
                    unless
it's through from below, with the feet rooted.
You must fight to keep full contact with the ground
or nothing will happen.
You stand there with arms cheering;
the ball dribbles away.

FROGS

Would intelligent frogs have invented the wheel,
or by extending the capacity for leaping
jumped directly to missiles?
Frog-life is discontinuous.
There's a lot of very serious dozing and staring,
then suddenly they're someplace else.
It's like poetry
or modern life.
They have wonderful voices
like a donkey, a power saw, and a monster banjo string
        combined.
They make noises that rule the night;
they answer each other.
If only frogs were intelligent
they'd be just like men.
They wouldn't live on flies and be eaten by snakes.
They'd drive out the snakes
and eat frogs.

IV

ELEVATION 800 FEET

The woods
crowd to the top of a high hill;
a basin of flowing light
is all around.
We descend to the sun
or live in sun at the top.
Outside at a long table
one tree blocks the direct
sun on my eyes;
masses of leaves,
oak, birch, weed, vine
tangle, shining, below me,
and under them the darkening hollows
are marked where a leaf gets sun.
Inviolate, humming on the air,
the picture of a broken child
passes the trees, recorded
for a million eyes.
The vines are not dying,
though this leaf is red
and that leaf falls
under our feet as we descend
the hill, the slipping road
under the woods
without people
but brown people, leaf city,
or instead loose stone
under our feet as we descend
cracking the leaves down, the air lovely.
Ants, she said,
what will they do?

They will hurry.
A cop walks by holding his stomach.
Blotches lie in the dust
on the wings of a butterfly.
Each night the screen glares.
The enemy in the background
has entered
a river
feeling the shame of towns
silting,
going out;
they hunt
where we have separated.
In a dusty room uptown,
downstream,
a girl paints a man.
Like the steel edge between two buildings
with knifeblade and thumb she presses him into her canvas;
low in her belly a stone presses the canvas.
I follow every stroke.
The man with the stiff-kneed stride
and his insides outside
wades on Moon Beach;
he falls backward, threatened by a steel beam;
he opens himself to the knife
on the walls of her room.
I see her on this page
the white mouthful of dreams;
each word is poker-faced with deceit.
What is happening, what has really happened?
Silver light flew to us over the park.
Or summer twilight, the lights coming on,
new money moist and gentle in the windows,
a soft dust falling over many bodies,

the answering excitement
to her bitchery.
I am divided
among many images.
Everything is alive but a little on edge.
The birds are working fiercely through the bushes;
nuts pop from the tree;
there is a steady hurried flying toward the light at sunset;
a squirrel runs
through a high branch.
We are warm, peaceful,
ready to kill only small things,
liking wine, streams, clearness.
The mortars softly
climbing and falling back;
we climb back
northward, inland
many years.
To have gone through it—
no bridge across the river for a thousand miles
south of Nanking.
A poet is like a set of silverware
used at a family dinner;
what happens where there is no meat,
no family?
What happens as the birds fly in at sunset
and the news comes on?
The garbage fire has gone down behind the house,
a steak broils on the porch;
a dark gentle poem is in me: a man moves forward quietly
        on all fours;
he is in a tunnel, he is naked, his calves are hurting;
the ground is like hard muscle and fur under his hands.
What happens, what is really happening?

Nothing is like what we say.
These words are not things but these
leaves are not things, these moments
are unfixed
that is like the rhythm of the crickets,
the bee
is unsteady
coming close to the page
and away.
By symmetry we move
through powerful wastes
to which also
we must reawaken.
I am a radio-television tree alarm clock
tuned to all the bands at once!
I wake up, flapping my arms, "Pine trees,
millionaires, sun-ball, proteins, brothers,
Cervantes, Moscow, hear me!"
This is a dream—to be on fire
with iron and sorrow and leaves.
Summerfilled, leaf-green, end of the world of summer,
blazing, particular sky,
I never loved her, my instinct was to ruin her.
Spasms of style.
These words are not things
but living in the country
has begun to teach me waste and miracle
walking downhill
for the milk, for the mail
something escapes me;
these weeds are not the rhythm but it is
like rhythm
walking downhill
part of the dead modern era

dust in the fluids of each cell
patterned like the markings on a butterfly
waste and miracle
each step
breaking the compost down.